THE AMAZING SOCIAL LIVES OF AFRICAN ELEPHANTS

BY SAMANTHA S. BELL

Published by The Child's World®
1980 Lookout Drive • Mankato, MN 56003-1705
800-599-READ • www.childsworld.com

Photographs ©: Vadim Nefedov/iStockphoto, cover, 1; Red Line Editorial, 5; Shutterstock Images, 6, 9; Jonathan Pledger/Shutterstock Images, 8; EcoPrint/Shutterstock Images, 10; Steve Bower/Shutterstock Images, 13; Tabby Mittins/Shutterstock Images, 14; Nobby Clarke/Shutterstock Images, 16; Grobler du Preez/Shutterstock Images, 17; Four Oaks/Shutterstock Images, 18; Johan Swanepoei/Shutterstock Images, 20

ISBN 9781503816268

LCCN 2016945596

Printed in the United States of America
PA02319

TABLE OF CONTENTS

FAST FACTS

Names

- African **savanna** elephant (*Loxodonta africana*)
- African forest elephant (*Loxodonta cyclotis*)

Diet

- African elephants feed on roots, grasses, fruit, flowers, and bark.
- They can eat up to 300 pounds (136 kg) in a single day.

Average Life Span

- Approximately 70 years

Size

- Approximately 10.5 feet (3.2 m) tall at the shoulder for males
- Approximately 8 feet (2.4 m) tall at the shoulder for females

Weight

- Up to 15,000 pounds (6,804 kg) for males
- Up to 8,000 pounds (3,629 kg) for females

Where They're Found

- Grassland savannas and open woodlands in central and southern Africa

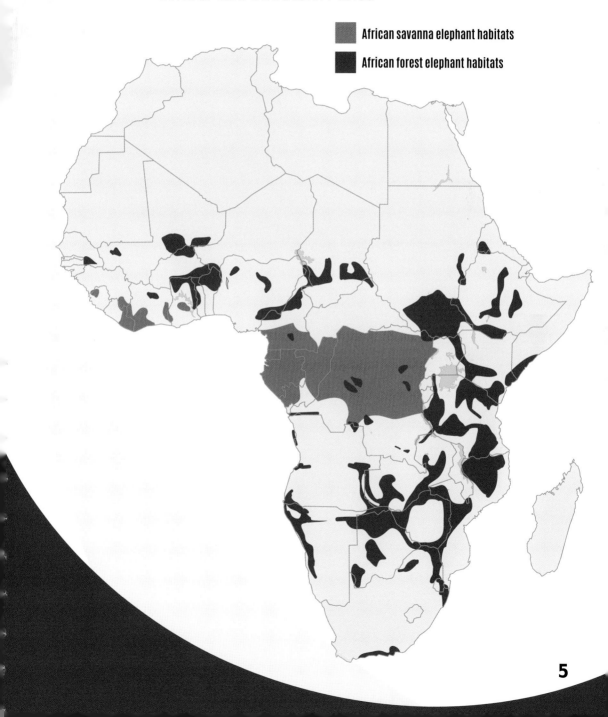

African savanna elephant habitats

African forest elephant habitats

Chapter 1

FOLLOWING THE LEADER

A group of elephants roams the African savanna. They use their long trunks to pull up grass and put it in their mouths. Suddenly, the oldest and biggest female stops. A lion is roaring in the distance.

The female elephant is the **matriarch**. She listens to the roar. She knows it is a male lion. It might attack. The matriarch lets out a low rumble. It is time to leave. The other elephants follow her in a single-file line.

The group of elephants is called a *herd*. A herd is a large family. There are ten other elephants in this family. Most are the matriarch's daughters and granddaughters. These elephants will be in the herd their whole lives.

◀ **The matriarch is often the biggest elephant in the herd.**

▲ African elephant herds often move in
single-file lines. This helps keep the
young elephants safe.

There are also a few young male elephants, or bulls.
They will leave the herd when they are 10 to 12
years old.

Since the matriarch is the oldest, she knows more
than the others. She remembers the best places to
find food and water. She leads the herd to a grove of
thorn trees.

The elephants start to **forage** again. They pull leaves and twigs from the trees. The elephants use their **tusks** to scrape bark off trees and dig up roots. The family spends much of the day eating. But the matriarch is always on the look out. She knows what **predators** to watch for. She keeps the herd safe.

▲ African elephants use their trunks to reach tree branches.

Chapter 2

A NEW BABY

One of the elephants is going to have a **calf**. The baby elephant has grown inside its mother for 22 months. The mother stays close to the herd. She gives birth to a bull. The baby elephant is already 3 feet (1 m) tall. He weighs approximately 200 pounds (91 kg).

The matriarch sees the calf. She raises her trunk and lets out a loud **trumpet**. She goes to meet the new baby. The other elephants in the herd rush over, too. The elephants surround the new calf to keep him safe. Then they help him stand up. The baby must stand to **nurse** from his mother.

The calf starts walking soon after he is on his feet. But he cannot see well. The mother hums to her baby.

◄ Female elephants can give birth once every five years.

The baby knows his mother's sound. He also knows her smell and touch.

The calf stays close to his mother. But the mother is not the only one watching over him. Older female elephants help raise the baby. They have more experience. Younger female elephants also take care of the calf. They are called *allomothers*. They are learning how to be mother elephants.

The new calf already knows how to nurse. He also knows how to follow his mother. But he learns everything else by watching the other elephants in the family.

The calf practices using his trunk. There are about 100,000 muscles in his trunk. The baby must learn how to control them. He watches his mother pick up grass and sticks. The calf tries to pick up sticks, too. He also uses his trunk to feel, sniff, and reach.

The calf learns about food. He starts trying to eat solid food when he is three months old. Sometimes he reaches his trunk into another elephant's mouth.

▲ Calves socialize through play.

This is how the calf learns what good food tastes and smells like.

The calf plays with other young elephants. They **romp** around and shake their heads. They toss sand in the air. Older elephants play with the baby, too. They lie on the ground. They let the calf climb on them.

Chapter 3

STRENGTH IN NUMBERS

The elephant family visits a watering hole. The elephants go into the water to cool off. The matriarch looks out for predators, such as lions and hyenas. She knows a watering hole can be a dangerous place.

Suddenly, the water ripples. A crocodile! The matriarch lifts her head and ears. She lets out a short snort and a rumble. The other elephants answer with soft rumbles. They listen and look at the crocodile. Then they surround the calf to protect him.

The group of elephants starts to move toward land. They all take a few steps. Then they stop. They smell the air. They lift their wide ears and listen.

◄ An elephant sucks water up with its trunk. Elephants drink by spraying water out of their trunks and into their mouths.

▲ **African elephants group together for protection.**

The crocodile is coming closer. The elephants move a little more. Then they stop and smell again. They know the crocodile is behind them now. The elephants continue moving in this way until they reach the shore. The baby makes it safely out of the water.

The calf lets out a cry. He still depends on the other elephants. The mother elephant comforts the calf.

She rubs her trunk over the baby's head. She gently rubs his back and belly. She makes low rumbling noises. These help the calf calm down. Family members use their trunks to comfort each other, too.

▲ Young elephants depend on bigger elephants to protect them from predators such as crocodiles.

Chapter 4

FAMILY LIFE

One of the elephants is not with the herd. The matriarch makes a sound so low that people cannot hear it. The sound moves through the ground. The lost elephant feels the vibrations in her feet. She lifts her head and calls back.

The two elephants call back and forth. Finally, the herd finds the lost elephant. The elephants flap their ears and spin around. They rumble in celebration.

A group of bull elephants is nearby. The bulls are traveling together. The younger ones learn from the older ones. When the females are ready to mate, they call to the bulls. After mating, the bulls move away again.

◄ African elephants' feet can sense small vibrations in the ground.

▲ Elephant families sometimes socialize with one another.

The herd meets another elephant family. The two families greet each other. They trumpet and scream. Other herds come, too. Soon there are 50 elephants together.

Not far from the group, an elephant lies on the ground. The elephant is hurt. Other elephants try to feed her. Some try to lift her with their tusks. They guard her from other animals. But the elephant dies.

The family uses their feet and tusks to cover the body with sand.

The herd **mourns**. Some elephants stay with the body for days. Even after many years have passed, they will still remember the elephant that has died. Some will pause where the elephant died. Others will touch the bones with their feet or trunks.

The matriarch decides it is time to go. She leads the family to a new place to eat, drink, and rest. Another elephant in the herd will soon give birth. The family will be celebrating again.

THINK ABOUT IT

- Elephants are good at communicating. How does it help them survive?
- In what ways is an elephant family like a human family?
- Some people say, "An elephant never forgets." From what you have read, what does this mean?

GLOSSARY

calf (KAF): A calf is a baby elephant. The calf follows his mother to the river.

forage (FOR-ij): To forage is to search for food. An elephant will forage for most of the day.

matriarch (MAY-tree-ark): A matriarch is a female who rules or dominates a family. The elephants follow a matriarch.

mourns (MORNS): A person or animal mourns by showing sadness when another has died. An elephant herd mourns in many ways.

nurse (NURS): To nurse is to drink milk from one's mother. The elephant calf will nurse for five years.

predators (PRED-uh-turs): Predators are animals that kill and eat other animals. Elephants protect their young from predators.

romp (RAHMP): To romp is to play in a noisy and rough way. Baby elephants romp with each other.

savanna (suh-VAN-uh): A savanna is a grassland with scattered trees. Some African elephants live on the African savanna.

trumpet (TRUM-pit): To trumpet means to make a loud, sharp sound. Elephants trumpet when they are excited.

tusks (TUSKS): Tusks are long teeth used for digging for food or as weapons. Sometimes an elephant's two tusks are different sizes.

TO LEARN MORE

Books

Blewett, Ashlee Brown, and Daniel Raven-Ellison. *Mission: Elephant Rescue*. Washington, DC: National Geographic, 2014.

Joubert, Beverly, and Dereck Joubert. *Face to Face with Elephants*. Washington, DC: National Geographic, 2008.

O'Connell, Caitlin. *A Baby Elephant in the Wild*. New York: Houghton Mifflin Harcourt, 2014.

Web Sites

Visit our Web site for links about African elephants: childsworld.com/links

Note to Parents, Teachers, and Librarians: We routinely verify our Web links to make sure they are safe and active sites. So encourage your readers to check them out!

SELECTED BIBLIOGRAPHY

Barcus, Christy Ullrich. "What Elephant Calls Mean: A User's Guide." *National Geographic*. National Geographic Society, 2016. Web. 4 Apr. 2016.

"Echo: An Elephant to Remember: Elephant Emotions." *PBS Nature*. WNET, 11 Oct. 2010. Web. 11 Apr. 2016.

"Elephants Learn from Others." *ElephantVoices*. ElephantVoices, 2016. Web. 8 Apr. 2016.

Safina, Carl. *Beyond Words: What Animals Think and Feel*. New York: Henry Holt, 2015. Print.

INDEX

ABOUT THE AUTHOR

Samantha S. Bell has written more than 35 nonfiction books for children. Animals are one of her favorite topics to write about. She earned her bachelor's degree and teaching certification from Furman University. She is a workshop and conference speaker, creative writing teacher, and enthusiastic student of all things nature.